HAPPINESS
QIGONG

HAPPINESS QIGONG

Course Workbook

Robert Peng

Rainbow Tree Publishing

New York

Happiness Qigong Workbook
Rainbow Tree Publishing, New York

Copyright © 2011 by Jihui Peng

All rights reserved, including the rights to reproduce this book or portions thereof in any form whatsoever without the prior written permission of Rainbow Tree Publishing, except where permitted by law.

First softcover edition published 2011
Printed in the United States of America

ISBN: 978-1-4565445-6-0

Author: Robert Peng
Editor & layout design: Rafael Nasser
Cover and interior art: Tobin Dorn

The photos in this book are by Ramon Fernandez

The information contained in this book is intended to be educational. The authors and publishers are in no way liable for any misuse of the information. Please consult with a qualified medical advisor before practicing the exercises described in this book if you have any health-related conditions.

For more information about special discounts for bulk purchases or any other queries, please contact rainbow.tree.publishing@gmail.com.

This book is printed on acid-free paper.

www.RobertPeng.com

This book belongs to

───────────────────────────────

Contents

Preface 1

PART 1 - BASIC THEORY
The Three Dantians 4
The 7 Dantian Types 6
The 4 Golden Wheels 14
The Three Treasures 18
Nourishing Qi 18
Awakening Awareness 20

PART 2 - ESSENTIAL PRACTICES
Three Treasures Standing Meditation 24
Lotus Meditation 34
Connecting Universe 48
Changing Brandy into Cognac 72

PART 3 - PRACTICE GUIDELINES
Practice Log 76
My Notes 80
Additional Resources 86
Workshop and Classes 90
About Robert Peng 94

Preface

Flipping through the pages of this workbook you will notice that it contains pictures of the featured exercises taught in the workshop entitled, *Happiness Qigong*, and lots of empty space for note taking. With the exception of this page, words are as sparse as fruit trees in a desert. I encourage you to transform the barren lines in the pages that follow into a forest of instructions that you can refer to in the future.

    Ironically, when I was young, Xiao Yao, my Qigong Master, discouraged me from taking notes when he taught me a new practice. So why would I steer you in the opposite direction?

    I had the opportunity to practice Qigong with Xiao Yao every day. He was always there to correct my mistakes and to add more details when my practiced improved. But we will only be together for a brief period of time during which I will impart many nuanced ideas and details. This workbook will continue to be your trusty guide after we part ways. (You may also rely on additional study aids to support your progress—the book *Qigong Master* and its companion CD and DVD sets.)

    When taking notes realize that Qigong practice unfolds in three stages. The first stage consists of learning the physical movements of the exercise. You might be standing, sitting, or moving around. The body mechanics of a practice establish its foundation.

    The second element consists of the breathing pattern and visualization. *What should you be doing with your mind while you are exercising your body?* The answer to this question defines the psychological level of Qigong practice.

    Finally, once you *bodymind* is coordinating its action smoothly, the energetic dimension comes into awareness. At this stage you realize the essence of the practice. When you perceive Qi flowing through your bodymind, an exercise transforms into Qigong. This is the goal towards which the arrow points.

    May Qigong practice bring you *Peace* and *Happiness*.

Good Qi,
Robert Peng

PART 1

BASIC THEORY

The Three Dantians

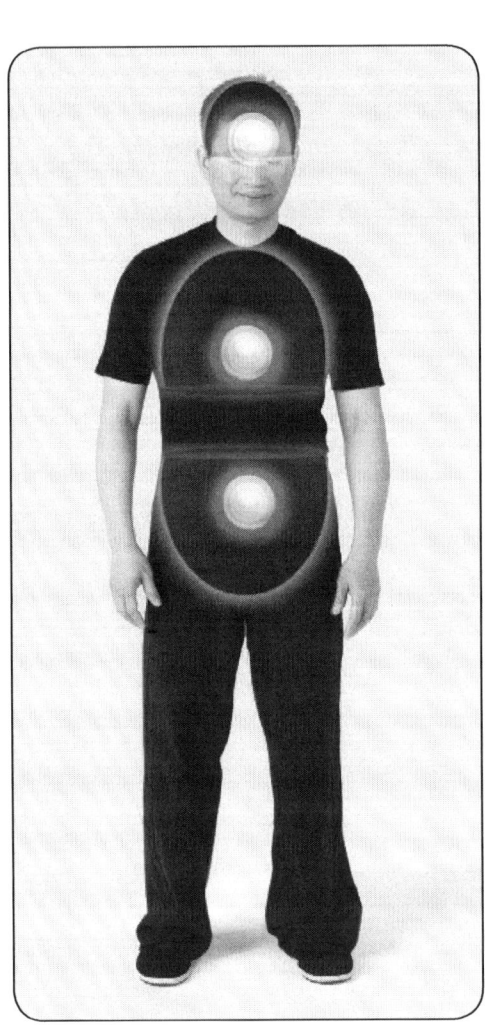

The Three Dantians	Attributes When Strong	Attributes When Weak
Upper Dantian		
Middle Dantian		
Lower Dantian		

The 7 Dantian Types

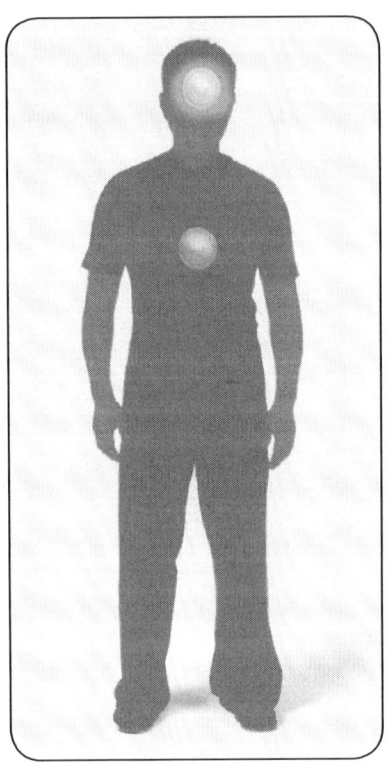

Type 1

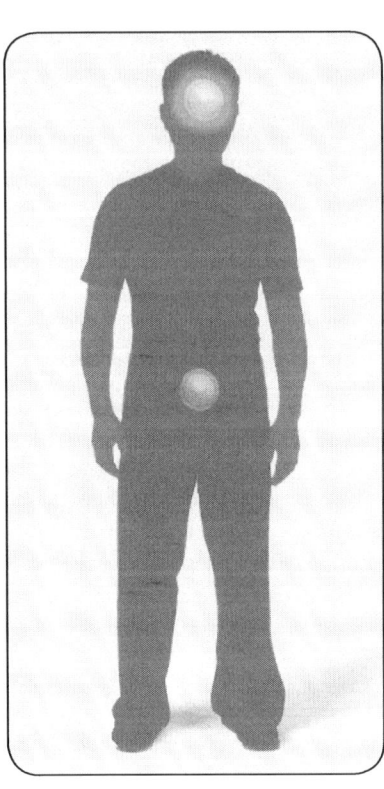

Type 2

BASIC THEORY

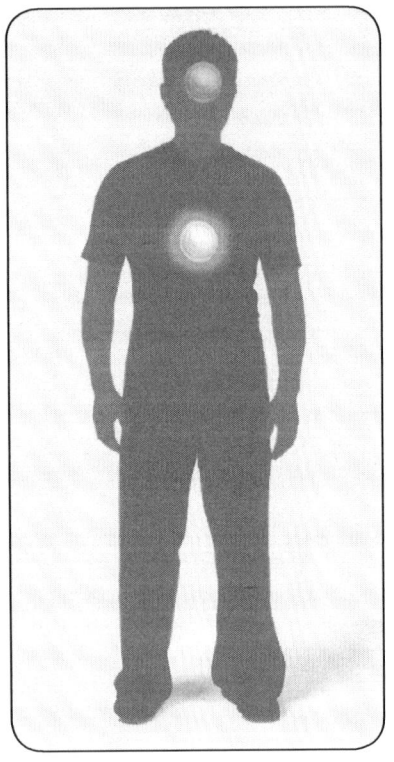

Type 3   Type 4

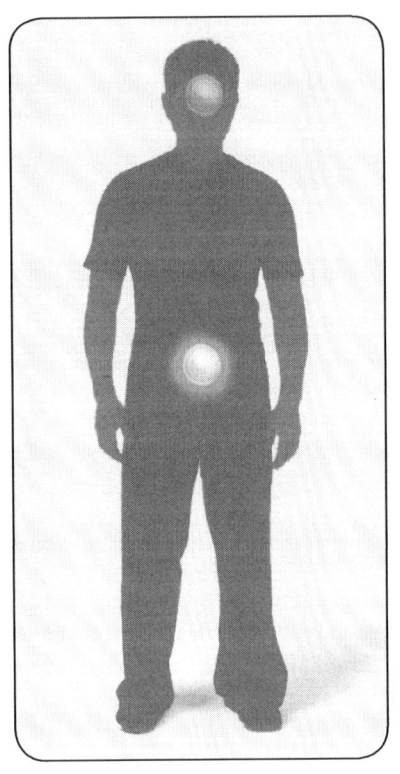

Type 5

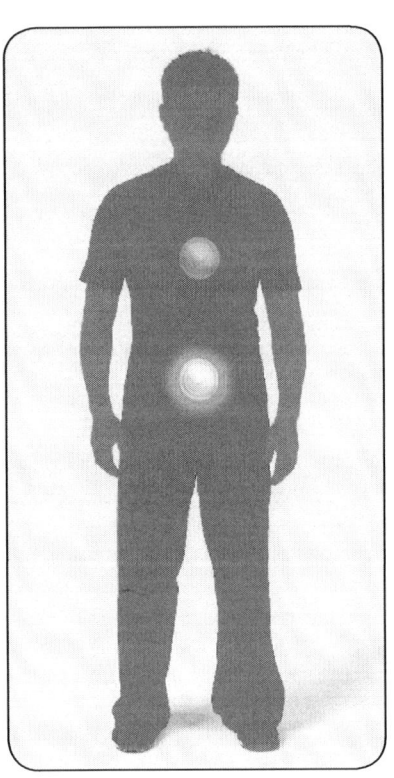

Type 6

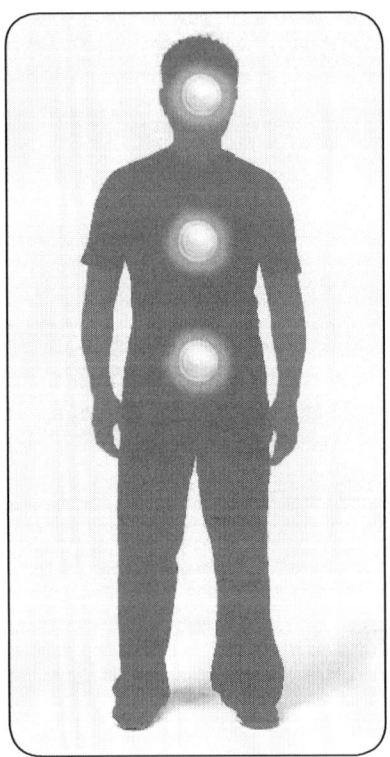

Type 7

BASIC THEORY

The 4 Golden Wheels

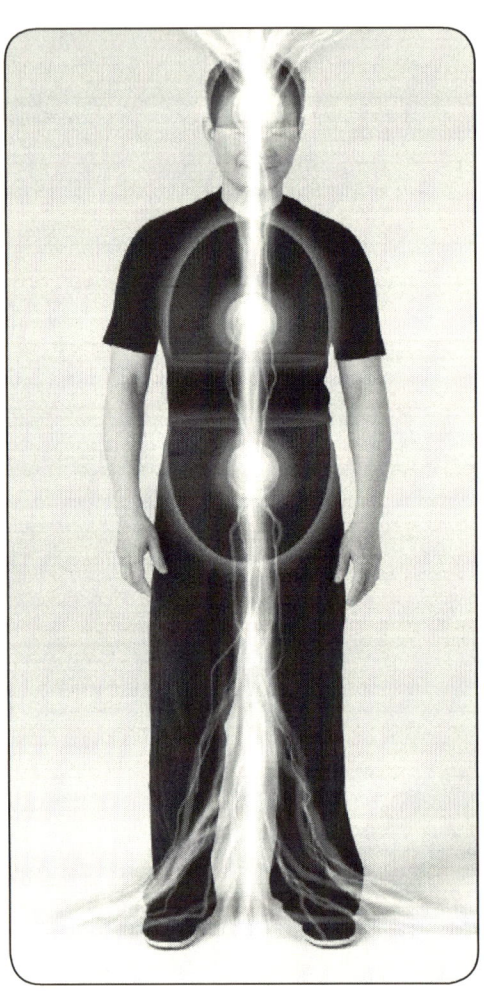

BASIC THEORY

The Three Treasures

The Three Treasures	Attributes When Strong	Attributes When Weak
HEAVEN QI *Sun* *Moon* *Stars*		
HUMAN QI *Upper Dantian (Shen)* *Middle Dantian (Qi)* *Lower Dantian (Jing)*		
EARTH QI *Fire* *Water* *Wind*		

Nourishing Qi

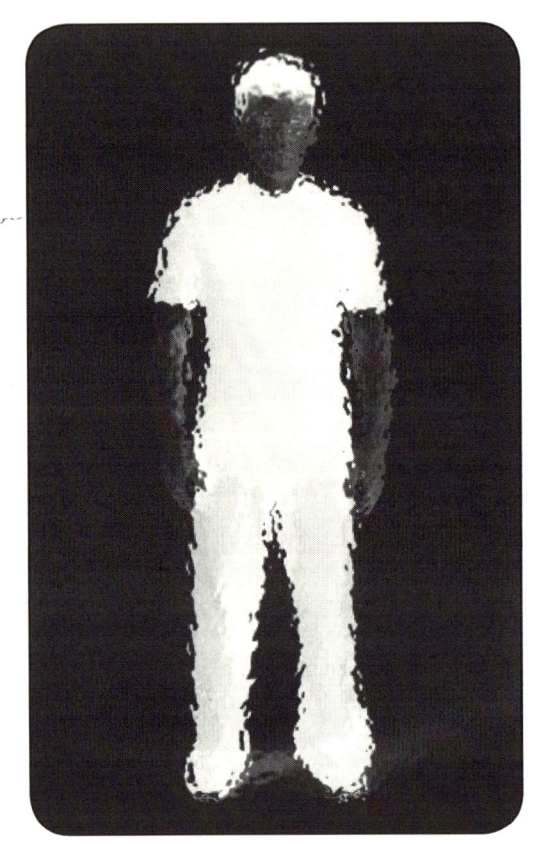

BASIC THEORY

Awakening Awareness

BASIC THEORY

PART 2

ESSENTIAL PRACTICES

Three Treasures Standing Meditation

STARTING POSTURE

ESSENTIAL PRACTICES

HEAVEN POSTURE

ESSENTIAL PRACTICES 27

EARTH POSTURE

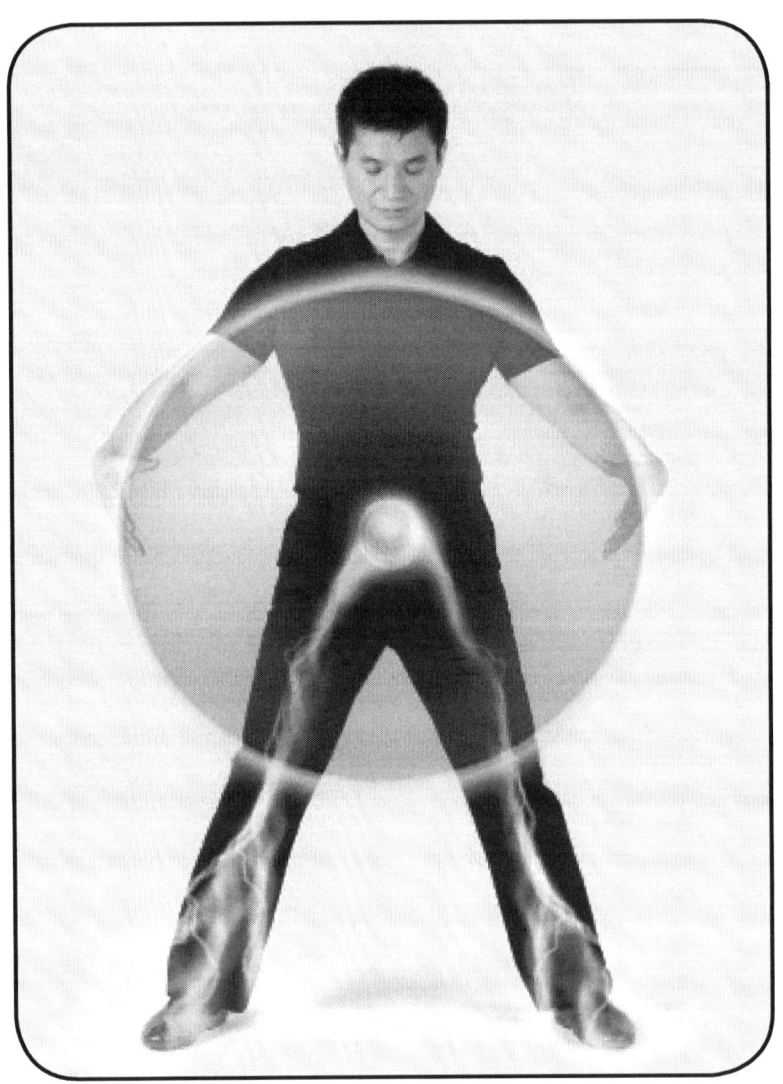

HUMAN POSTURE

UNIVERSAL POSTURE

ESSENTIAL PRACTICES

Lotus Meditation

ONG

AHH

HONG

ONG-AHH-HONG

PARTING FINGERS

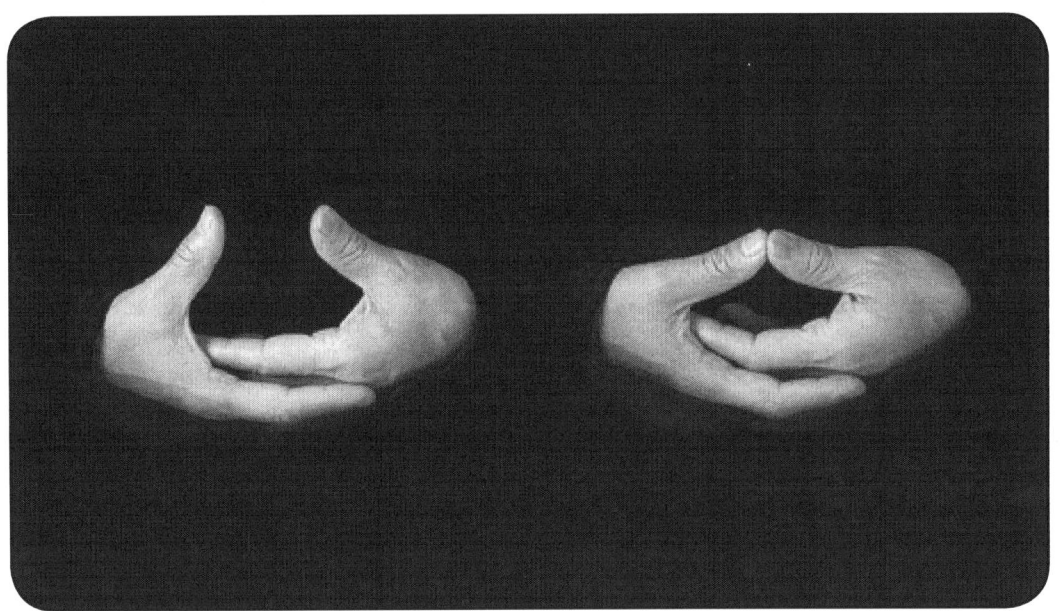

ESSENTIAL PRACTICES

FLOATING

UNDER THE WATERFALL

THE BEING OF LIGHT

ESSENTIAL PRACTICES   43

ENTERING THE HEART

FRAGRANCE OF THE LOTUS

THE LOTUS OPENS

HAPPINESS RISES

ESSENTIAL PRACTICES

Connecting Universe

LEFT SIDE HORIZONTAL

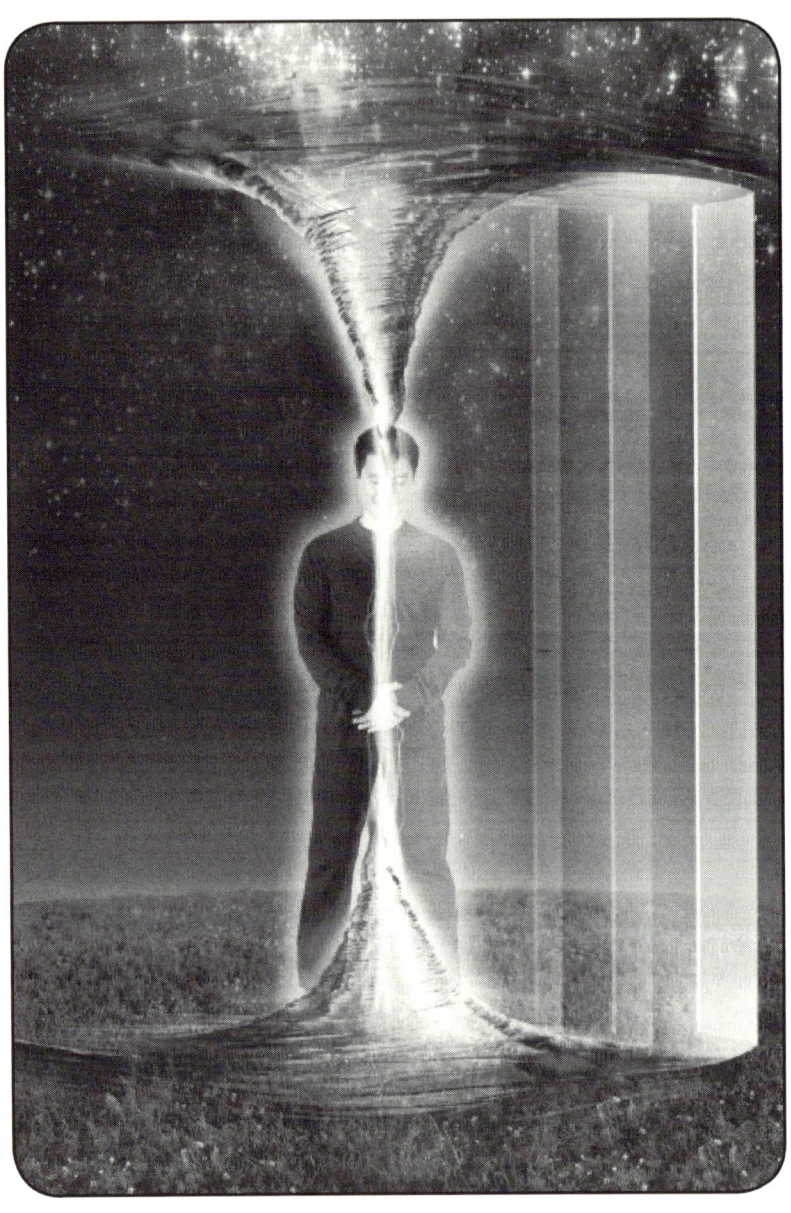

REVERSE DIRECTIONS

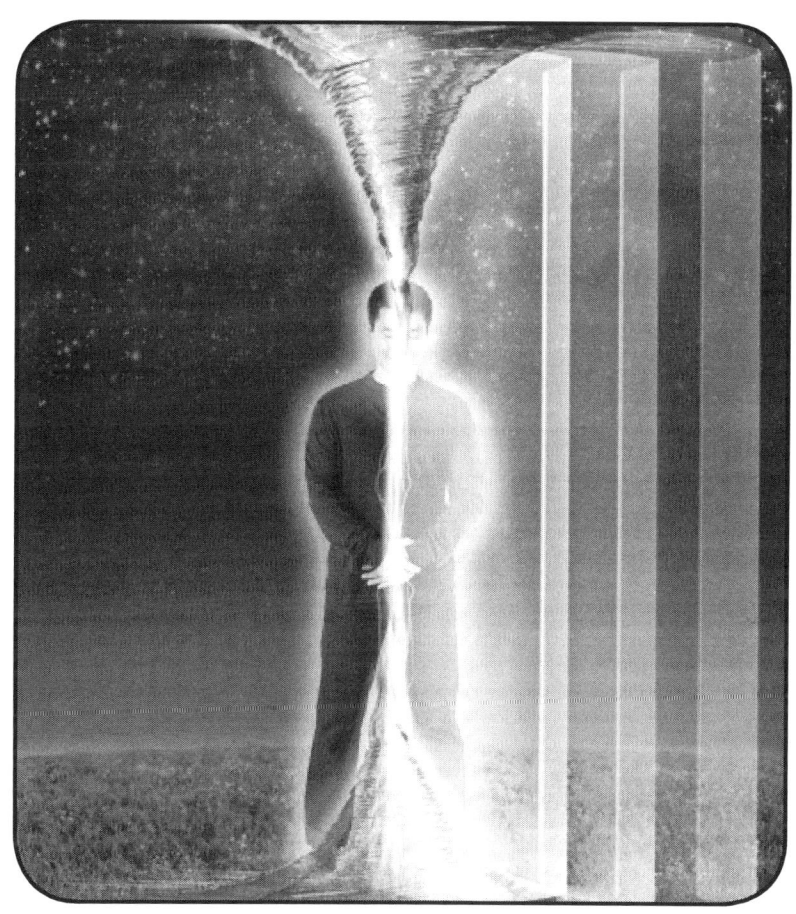

RIGHT SIDE HORIZONTAL

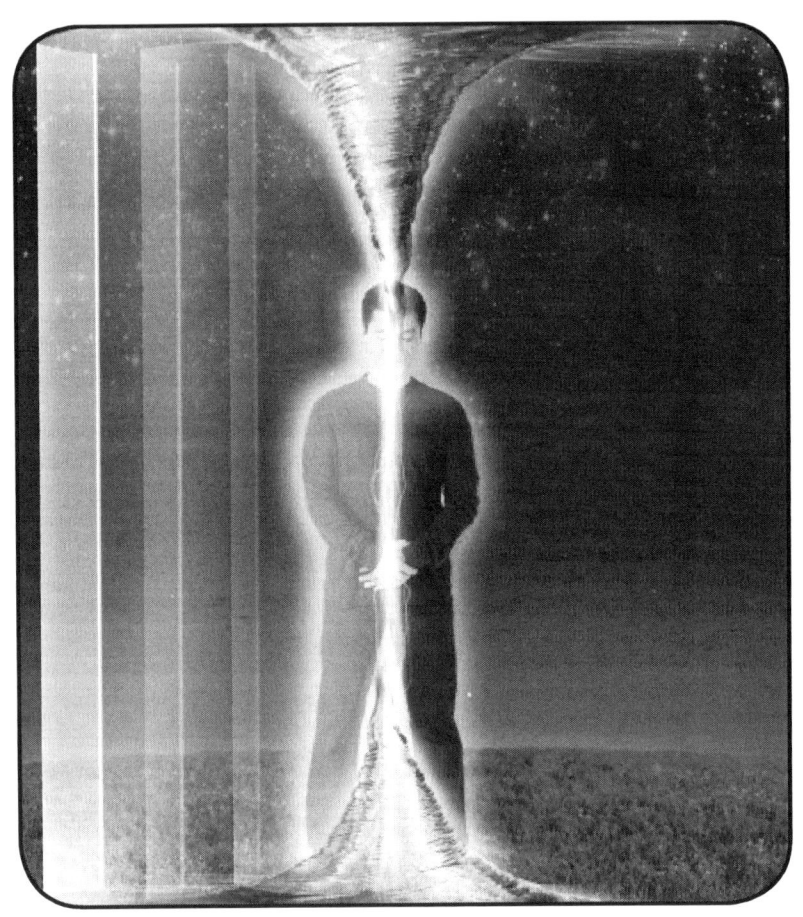

REVERSE DIRECTIONS

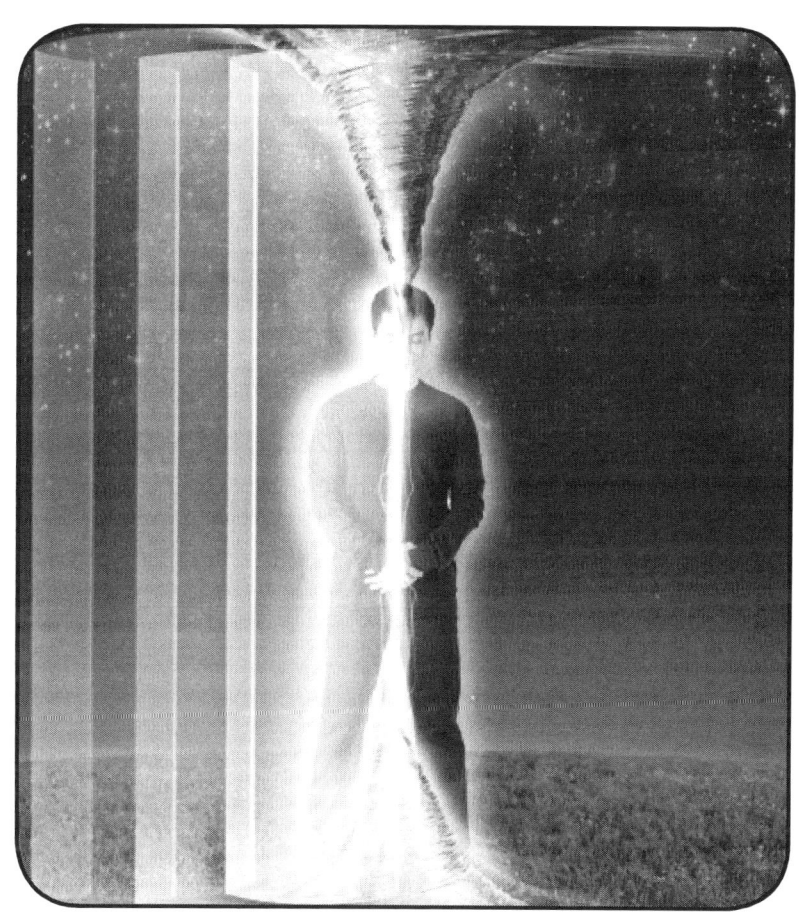

FRONT HALF HORIZONTAL

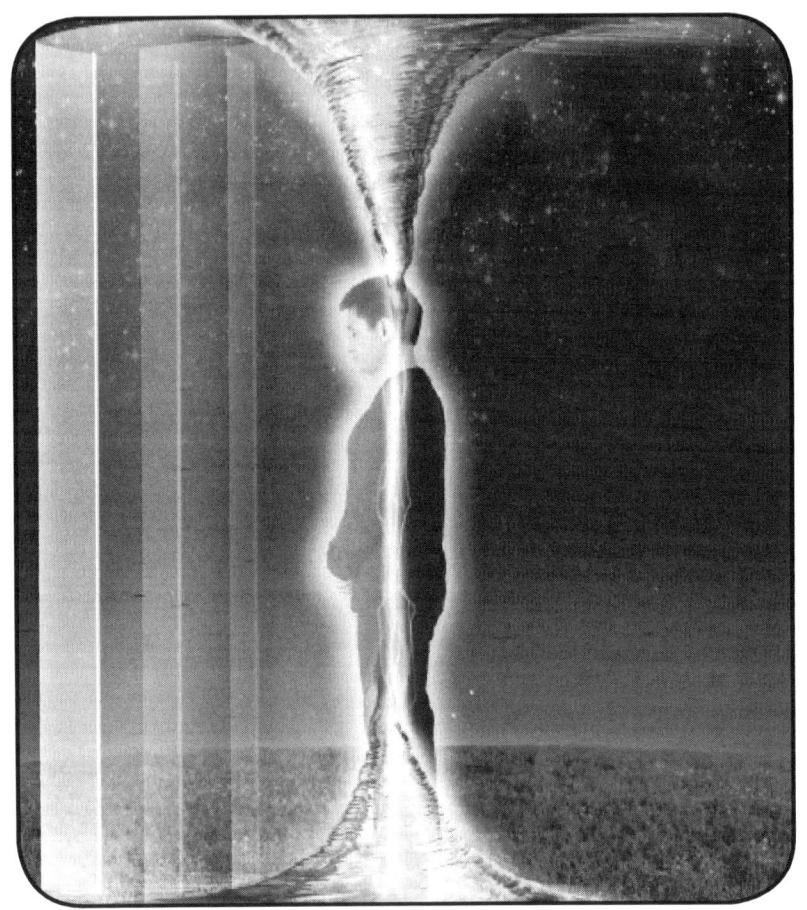

REVERSE DIRECTIONS

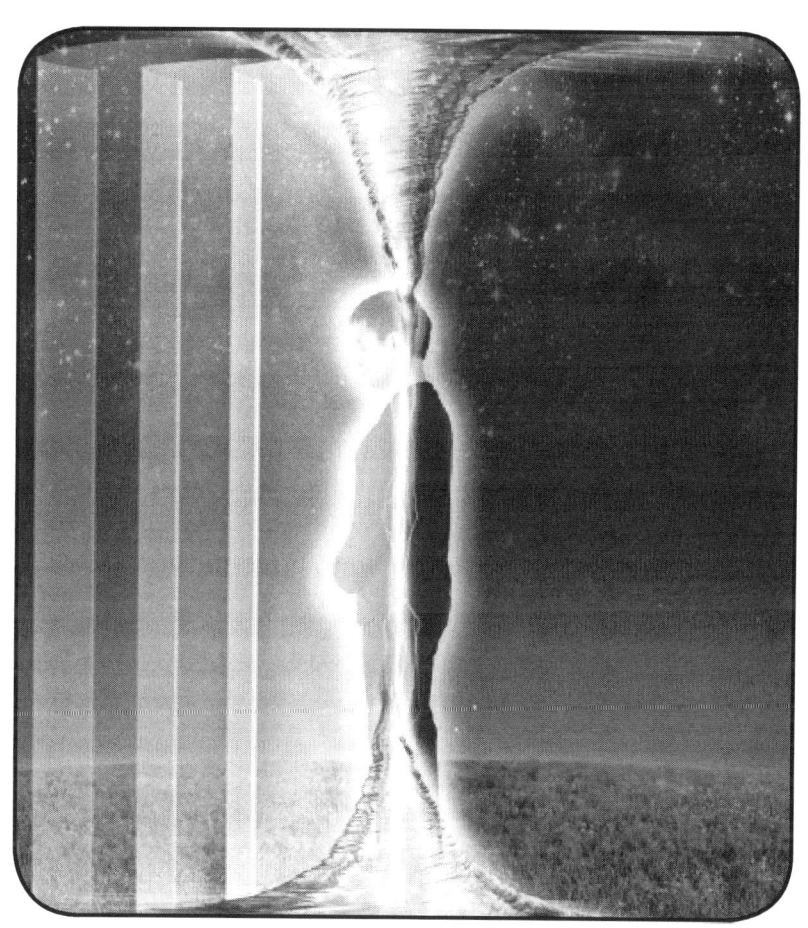

BACK HALF HORIZONTAL

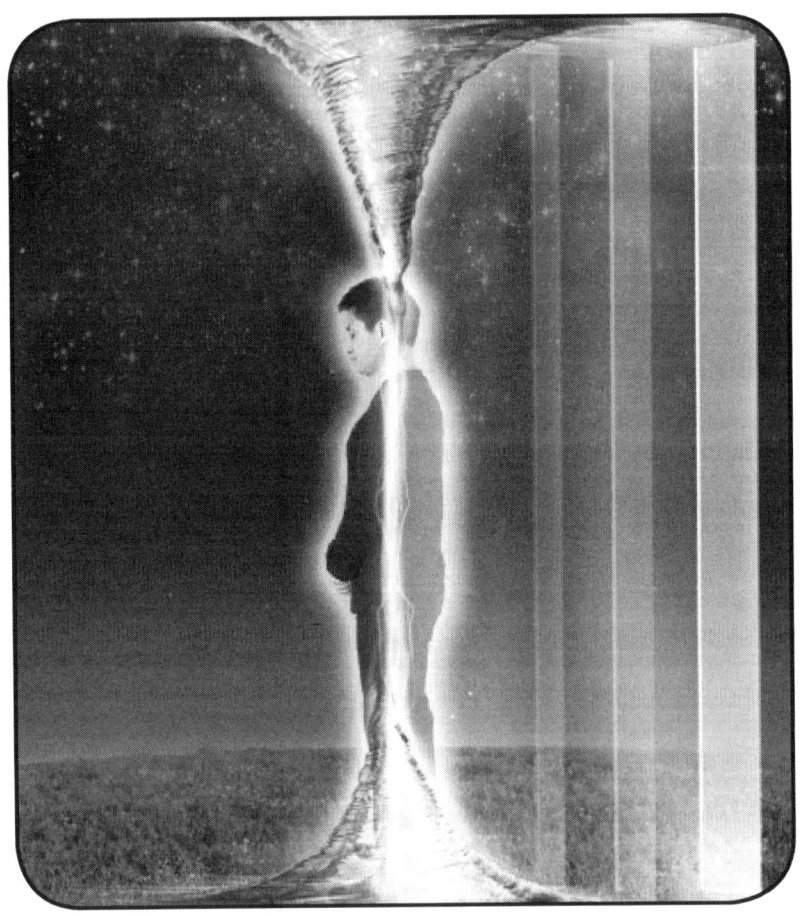

REVERSE DIRECTIONS

MY NOTES

LEFT SIDE VERTICAL

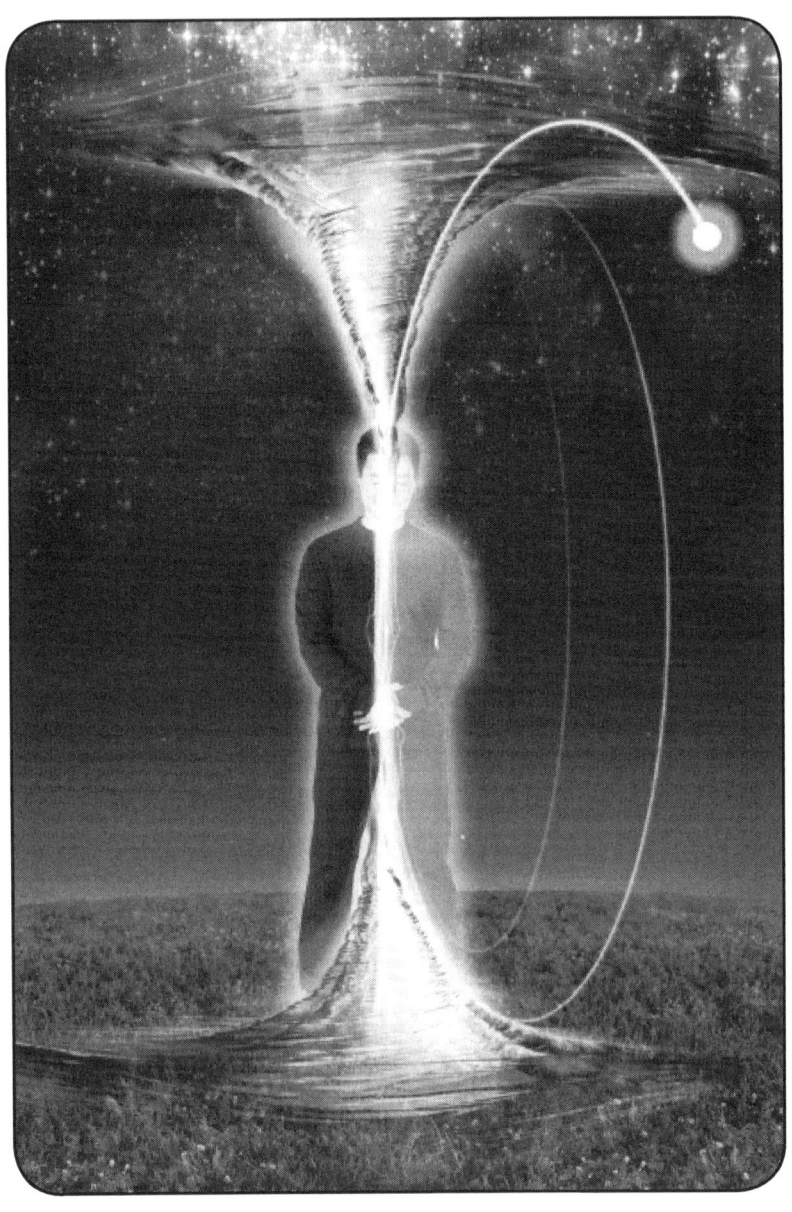

REVERSE DIRECTIONS

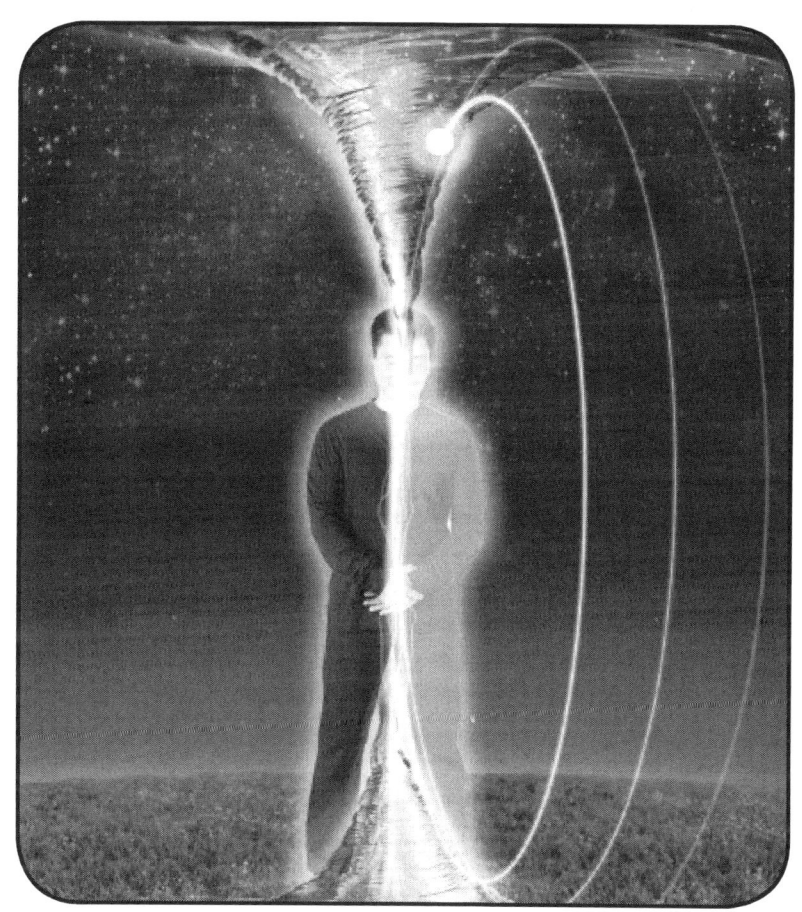

RIGHT SIDE VERTICAL

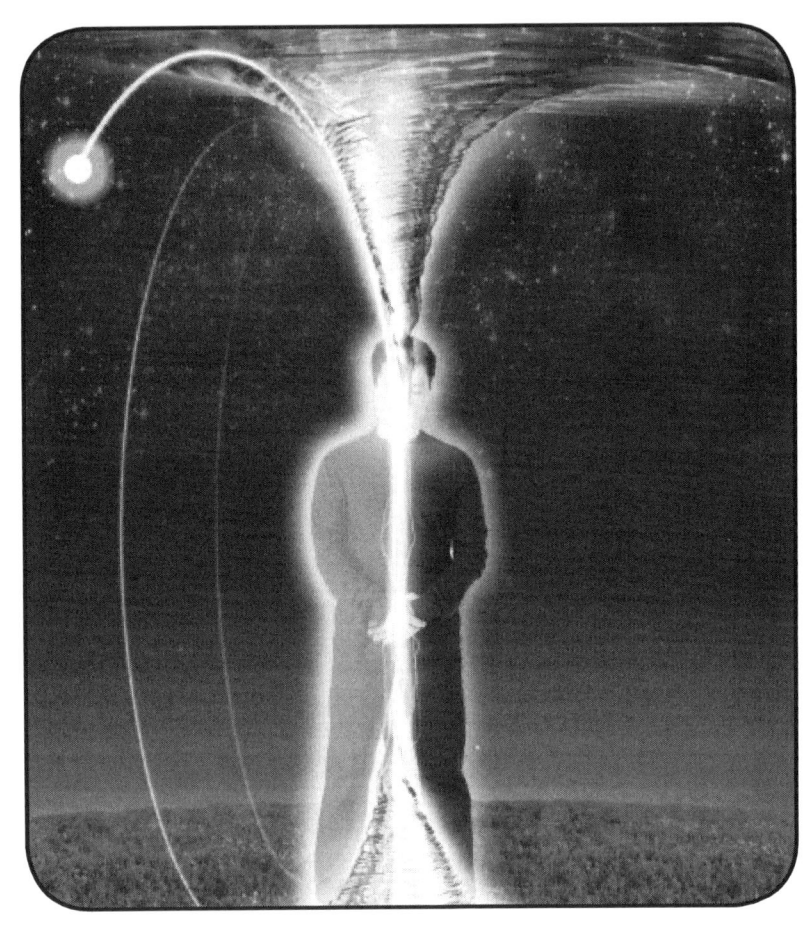

REVERSE DIRECTIONS

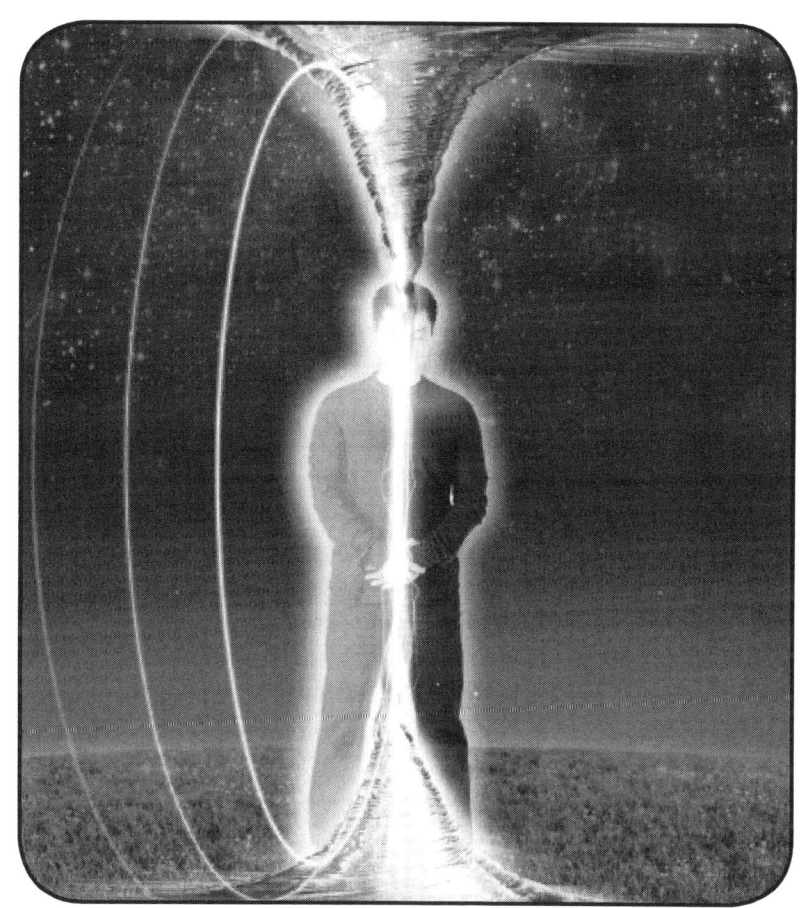

FRONT HALF VERTICAL

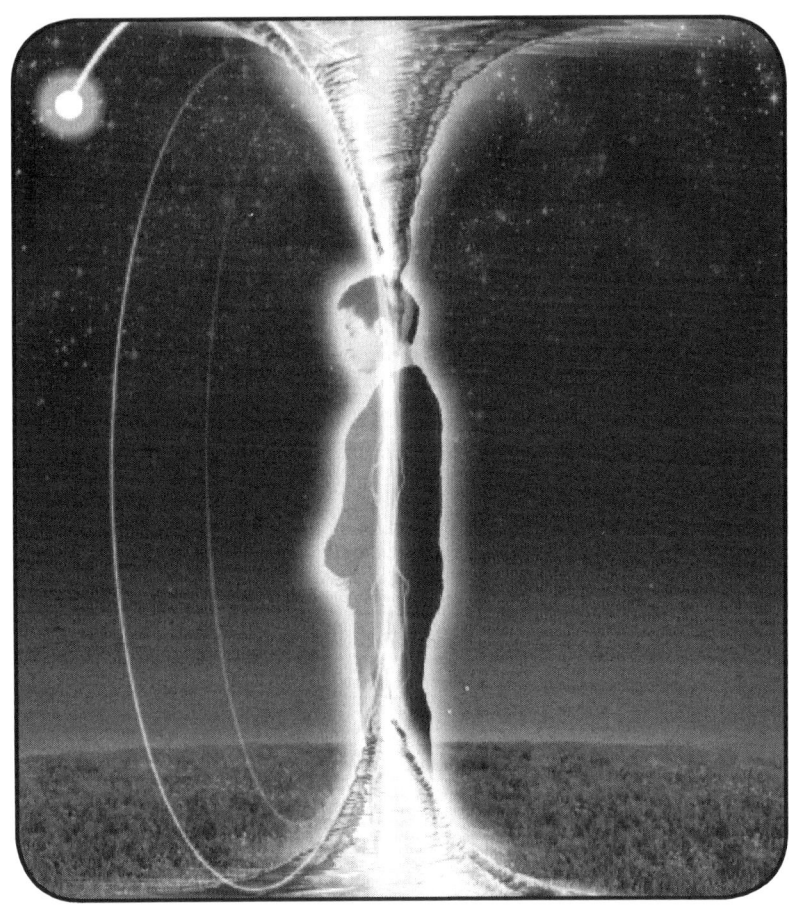

REVERSE DIRECTIONS

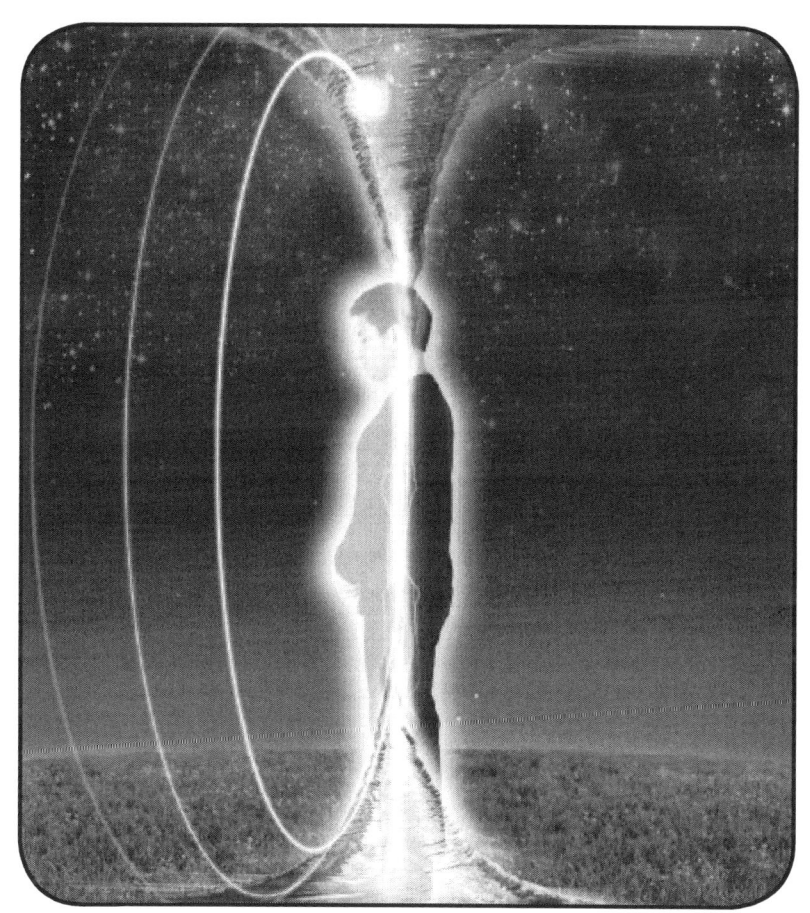

BACK HALF VERTICAL

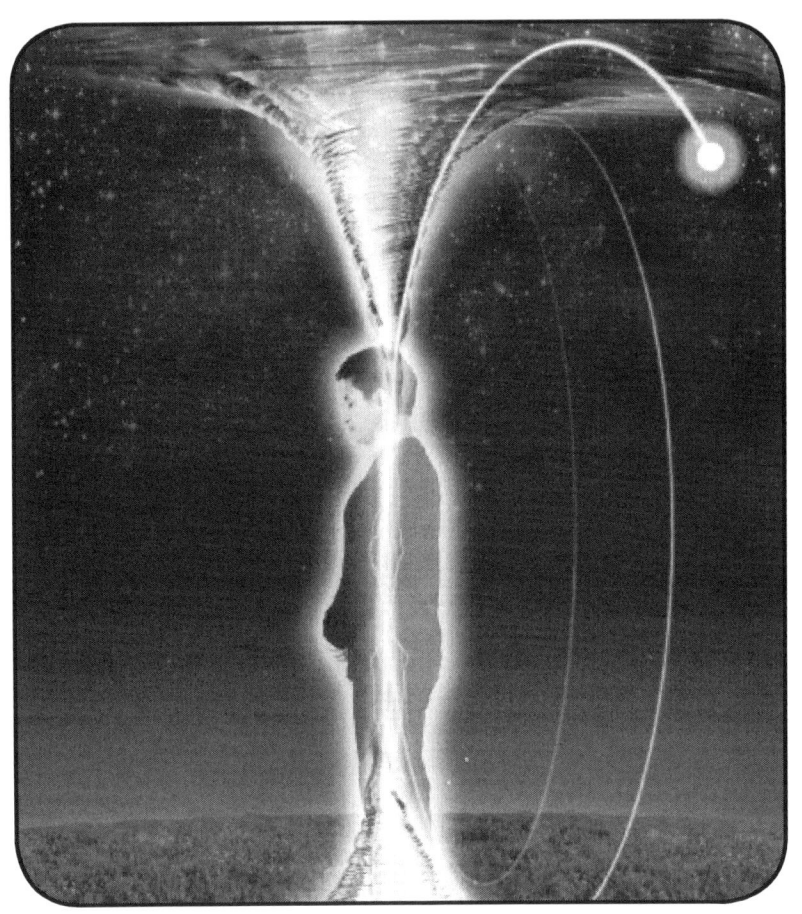

REVERSE DIRECTIONS

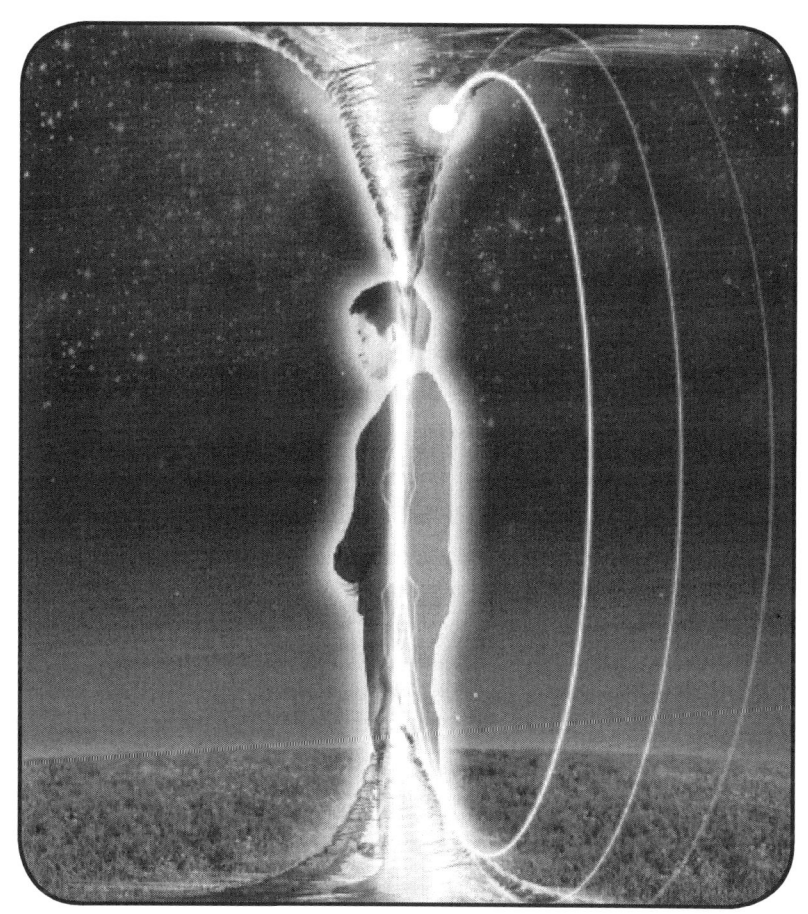

MY NOTES

CONCENTRIC CIRCLES

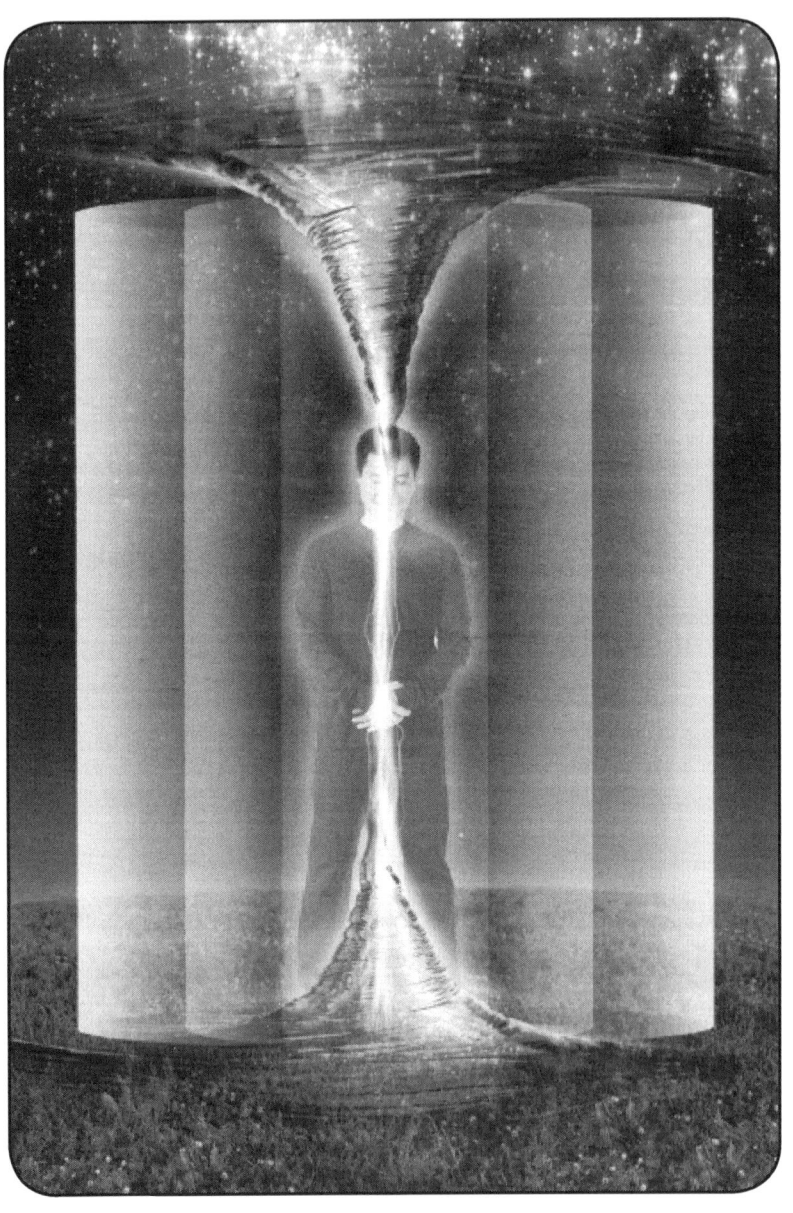

REVERSE DIRECTIONS

NOURISH YOUR QI

ESSENTIAL PRACTICES

Changing Brandy Into Cognac

ESSENTIAL PRACTICES

PART 3

PRACTICE GUIDELINES

Practice Log

First Month

Week 1	Day 1	Day 2	Day 3	Day 4	Day 5	Day 6	Day 7

Week 2	Day 1	Day 2	Day 3	Day 4	Day 5	Day 6	Day 7

Week 3	Day 1	Day 2	Day 3	Day 4	Day 5	Day 6	Day 7

Week 4	Day 1	Day 2	Day 3	Day 4	Day 5	Day 6	Day 7

Second Month

Week 1	Day 1	Day 2	Day 3	Day 4	Day 5	Day 6	Day 7

Week 2	Day 1	Day 2	Day 3	Day 4	Day 5	Day 6	Day 7

Week 3	Day 1	Day 2	Day 3	Day 4	Day 5	Day 6	Day 7

Week 4	Day 1	Day 2	Day 3	Day 4	Day 5	Day 6	Day 7

Third Month

Week 1	Day 1	Day 2	Day 3	Day 4	Day 5	Day 6	Day 7

Week 2	Day 1	Day 2	Day 3	Day 4	Day 5	Day 6	Day 7

Week 3	Day 1	Day 2	Day 3	Day 4	Day 5	Day 6	Day 7

Week 4	Day 1	Day 2	Day 3	Day 4	Day 5	Day 6	Day 7

My Notes

MY NOTES

MY NOTES

MY NOTES

ADDITONAL RESOURCES

Qigong Master, My Life and Secret Teachings

I am happy to announce that after three exciting years of hard work, my book, *QIGONG MASTER: My Life and Secret Teachings, is finally in print*. The book describes how I met my Master, Xiao Yao, a monk with extraordinary spiritual gifts. It recounts my spiritual adventures, including 100 day water fast I did as a teenager in a dark, underground chamber in a remote mountaintop monastery.

QIGONG MASTER conveys the essence of Qigong in simple terms through storytelling and visual imagery. The book contains an abundance of practical information, beautiful artwork, and enjoyable exercises that we can use to "upgrade" our life. The book also explores how Qigong principles can help us become healthier, more loving, and wiser, so that we can enhance our relationships and make our world a better place.

Endorsements are starting to stream in, and here is what people are saying:

Robert Peng's story is a miraculous journey into uncharted territory.
~Florence Comite, MD, Yale School of Medicine

Robert's story brought me immense joy, and I felt a deep sense of hope for everyone as I read the book.
~Nigol Koulajian, Board of Directors, Omega Institute

Robert's Qi helped save my life. But he does something more important than heal, he teaches you to heal yourself.
~Sally Jesse Raphael, Talk Show Host

About fifty pages into QIGONG MASTER, I began to feel a powerful desire to walk across the country just to listen to Robert Peng talk about anything - the weather, baseball, it would not matter. This man knows things. He is a living link to a tradition that could give new meaning to the word "human."
~Steven Forrest, author of The Inner Sky

To order a copy please visit www.RobertPeng.com.

88 HAPPINESS QIGONG

5 CD Companion Set to the Book Qigong Master

These five CDs are the audio companions to the book *QIGONG MASTER, My Life and Secret Teachings*. They can be ordered individually or as a box set.

EMPOWERMENTS (CD 1) - This CD features the Hologram Palm Empowerment of the Upper, Middle, and Lower Dantians, the Breathing Empowerment of the Central Meridian, and Awakening Awareness. These Qigong exercises are designed to awaken and strengthen your capacity for Wisdom, Love, Vitality, and Integrity. These are the basic elements that make up the flow of life and when all of them are activated and synchronized we experience inner harmony and an alignment with the Universe. Total running time is 55 minutes.

THREE TREASURES STANDING MEDITATION (CD 2) - Heaven, Earth, and the Human Being make up the Three Treasures and through this exercise you will learn to integrate your own personal Qi energies with the energies of Heaven and Earth by holding a series of static postures. This practice enables you to fuse your Wisdom, Love, and Vitality with the qualities of heavenly inspiration and earthy groundedness. When all Three Treasures are aligned and the energy between them flows harmoniously you develop greater willpower, focus, and intention. Total running time is 52 minutes.

4 GOLDEN WHEELS EXERCISE (CD 3) - There are three main Energy Centers called Dantians inside the body that store vast amounts of Qi energy. This practice relies on four different movement patterns to gently activate these Three Dantians and dissolve the energy blockages that keep you from actualizing your full potential. When Qi energy flow is restored, each Dantian becomes like a gurgling spring of fresh energy that streams smoothly into your activities. This exercise leaves you feeling rejuvenated, open, and ready to flow effortlessly through the day. Total running time is 54 minutes.

LOTUS MEDITATION (CD4) - In this beautiful guided visualization you take a journey to the source of divinely inspired love—the awakened heart. After completely cleansing your body by sitting under a purifying waterfall that is cascading healing energy down from the sky, you meet a Being of Light in a peaceful garden, absorb its essence, and then merge with it. Then you and the Being of Light merge with a beautiful lotus flower and radiate the fragrance of divine love. This practice awakens your compassion and deepens your capacity to experience the Universe as an unbounded sea of divine love. Total running time is 65 minutes.

CONNECTING UNIVERSE (CD5) - When our personal energy field is connected to the energy field of the Universe we feel at home in the cosmos and relate to everyone in it as a member of our extended family. In those moments when we experience this happy state we are filled with spiritual wellbeing. But when our energy field contracts and we disconnect from the Universe, we feel alone in a cold, vast, and uncaring world. Connecting Universe is a meditation practice that will help you build an energetic bond to the Universe strong enough to sustain you through challenging times. Total running time is 73 minutes.

To order the CDs please visit www.RobertPeng.com.

Workshops and Classes

The goal of Qigong is to establish peace and happiness as a way of life. Robert learned a practical method to embody this lofty ideal from his teacher, a humble monk named Xiao Yao, and now through Robert's workshops you can "download" this ancient knowledge in an enjoyable, practical, and clear format.

Every one of the workshops Robert teaches includes a series of Qigong practices designed to increase your inner power, help you regain youthful vitality, and optimize your flow state. Each course approaches these objectives from a slightly different angle and they all work together to create a powerful method to "upgrade" yourself.

You can start with any course and still benefit but we recommend that you begin by attending QIGONG EMPOWERMENTS. Here you will be introduced to the guiding principles of Robert's Qigong system and learn a set of exercises to "awaken" the *Energy Centers* that you will be working with in other courses.

QIGONG EMPOWERMENTS - *Awaken the 4 Golden Wheels*
Deep inside your body there exist three centers that hold vast amounts of Qi Energy in reserve. These three centers regulate your capacity for Wisdom, Love, and Vitality. In this workshop you will awaken these Energy Centers, empower, and harmonize them. The Qi energy activated in this workshop is the raw material that is further developed and refined in other workshops.

HAPPINESS QIGONG - *Exercise the 4 Golden Wheels*
This workshop offers the tools you need to integrate the qualities of Wisdom, Love, and Vitality. When these three qualities are brought into a balanced relationship you experience happiness gurgle up from the core of your being like a bubbling spring. The practices taught in this course form the bedrock of Robert Peng's Qigong system and by practicing them regularly happiness comes within your reach.

HARMONY QIGONG - *Flow like water*
When water flows it is pure and clear but when water stagnates it attracts disease. Compare a running stream and a stagnant pond. Which would you rather drink from? Similarly, when our "inner water"—our blood and our Qi Energy—flow smoothly, we radiate vibrant heath. But when stress tightens our bodies we form "logjams" around which symptoms appear and eventually disease forms. The practices taught in this workshop are designed to reestablish healthy internal flow through physical movement and meditation.

As our inner "waterways" stream along smoothly, we regain a sense of wellbeing and the rest of our body ecology thrives anew.

Guardian Qigong - *Unleash your inner power*
Guardian Qi is a thin layer of bio-energy that hugs the skin and protects the body from germs, emotional stress, and physical injury. When our Guardian Qi is strong our immune system is strong, emotional stress slides off harmlessly, and physical impact is less likely to leave behind a bruise. We feel protected. Under normal conditions Guardian Qi extends about two inches above the skin. By practicing Guardian Qigong you can double the density and double the height of its protective cover. The goal of this workshop is to boost the Guardian Qi around your body and also around your internal organs. When you unleash your inner power—both externally and internally—the world around you becomes a safer place, your spirit calms down, and your confidence grows.

Yi Jin Jing - *The Original Shaolin Exercise*
Over one thousand years ago an Indian monk by the name of Bodhidharma introduced Buddhism to China. According to legend, he found the bookish monks living in monasteries to be weak and lethargic. Believing that strong, healthy bodies enhance spiritual development he created the Yi Jin Jing, an exercise designed to strengthen sinews and integrate the body. The monks he taught this practice eventually became the legendary Shaolin fighting monks. In this workshop Robert reveals same twelve movement patterns that Bodhidharma taught the Shaolin monks. By practicing a special breathing technique, visualizations, and dynamic tension you too can develop steely strong sinews supercharged with Qi Energy.

12 Cycles Yang - *Revitalize your Yang body*
This course is a three month long process that begins with an *Opening session* and ends with a twenty four hour *Closing session*. During the Opening, Robert activates a series of energy points on each participant in preparation for the twelve exercises that are taught during this session. The exercises that make up 12 Cycles Yang focus on empowering the Yang or external part of the body. Using a unique breathing technique and rice bags, the practitioner concentrates Qi Energy into the Yang body and the internal organs. Gradually, the body and the mind transform, becoming stronger and more resilient.

At the Closing session Robert "seals" the energy points he activated in the Opening session, one meridian at the time. This process takes approximately twenty four hours. The course ends with a demonstration by the participants of their newfound Qigong powers. 12 Cycles Yang is open to anyone with a healthy mental and emotional state. The twelve exercises can be adjusted to suit body type, age, and physical disabilities. Some lifestyle changes are required of participants during the three months of practice, including no alcohol and sexual moderation.

12 Cycles Yin - *Revitalize your Yin body*

12 Cycles Yin complements 12 Cycles Yang and both courses work together as a unit to pack the whole body with Qi Energy. Although each course stands alone, we recommend first attending 12 Cycles Yang, although this is not a requirement. 12 Cycles Yin is a three month long process that begins with an *Opening session* and ends with a twenty four hour *Closing session.* During the Opening, Robert activates a series of energy points on each participant in preparation for the twelve exercises that are taught during this session. The exercises that make up 12 Cycles Yin focus on empowering the Yin or the vulnerable, inner parts of the body. Using a unique breathing technique (different from the technique taught in 12 Cycles Yang) and rice bags, the practitioner concentrates Qi Energy into the Yin body and the internal organs to strengthen them. At the Closing session Robert "seals" the energy points he activated in the Opening session, one meridian at the time. This process takes approximately twenty four hours. The course ends with a demonstration by the participants of their newfound Qigong powers. 12 Cycles Yin is open to anyone with a healthy mental and emotional state. The twelve exercises can be adjusted to suit body type, age, and physical disabilities. Some lifestyle changes are required of participants during the three months of practice, including no alcohol and sexual moderation.

Become a Qigong Healer - *Awaken your Healing Power*

This five part course introduces the Qigong healing techniques and meditations that Robert learned from his Master, Xiao Yao, a legendary monk with remarkable healing powers. Theory and practice are both covered in this hands-on workshop. Upon completion you will receive a signed certificate. The workshop is open to everyone.

Part 1: Power Palm, Sword FInger, Yin Yang Catch, Magic Palm, inviting Masters, Wogu psychic protection technique, "S" pattern energy clearing, Ever Spring Hand, Warm Qi vs. Cool Qi, Dian Xue technique for empowering the Central Meridian.

Part 2: Awakening the Third Eye, Qigong picture healing techniques, conducting Qi Energy, activating energy points by circling, tapping, and pressing and releasing, the Five Elements, QIgong hypnosis, introduction to major energy points.

Part 3: The 12 Meridians and major energy points (Part 1), hands-on healing practice.

Part 4: The 12 Meridians and major energy points (Part 2), hands-on healing practice.

Part 5: The 12 Meridians and major energy points (Part 3), the complete healing session. Review.

OTHER WORKSHOPS - *Deepen your Practice*

Ongoing Classes in New York City: Qigong classes are taught by Robert in New York City. These classes are open to everyone. Check *www.RobertPeng.com* for more information.

Good Morning Qigong, Good Evening Qigong: A lively morning and evening practice to get you ready for the day ahead and to calm you down before sleep.

Qigong for Seniors: Qigong is a gentle practice that can be done by anyone, regardless of age or physical condition. This workshop emphasizes simple exercises designed to energize the spirit and invigorate the body.

Retreats: The serene retreat atmosphere offers the opportunity to soak up the essence of Qigong at a leisurely pace, form lasting friendships, get to know Robert personally, and to deepen your practice.

Teacher Trainings: If you want to become a Qigong Instructor certified by Robert Peng or simply wish delve more deeply into the intricacies of the theory and practice, then the teacher *trainings offer you the opportunity to meet your needs.*

Other Services: To learn more about private classes, speaking engagements, or to sponsor Robert for a workshop, email *robertpengqigong@gmail.com*.

Robert Peng is a world-renowned Qigong Master who apprenticed secretly under a spiritually accomplished monk named Xiao Yao during the Chinese Cultural Revolution. Robert began by learning the martial arts and then the healing arts. As part of his training during his teen years he spent a hundred days in a dark, underground chamber without food.

During this period Xiao Yao visited him daily and instructed him in advanced practices intended to accelerate his spiritual development. As a result of doing the hundred-day fast and numerous other practices, Robert awakened extraordinary powers including the ability to discharge a concentrated form of Qi, or bio-energy, that feels like a strong electric current.

Xiao Yao encouraged Robert to pursue an academic degree and while Robert practiced Qigong with his Master behind closed doors, he also focused on his schoolwork. After completing high school, he pursued a degree in English Literature at Zhongnan University where he stayed on as a teacher after his graduation, ultimately becoming an assistant professor.

Robert's reputation as a Qigong healer and teacher spread while he taught English and in 1992 he resigned his post at the university to teach Qigong publicly on Hainan Island in Southern China which was the gateway to the West at the time. He opened the first Qigong healing clinic on the island along with another Qigong healer. Within a five year span they taught Qigong to over 150,000 students and did Qigong healing treatments on many prominent figures from the Western world.

In the mid 1990s, Robert was invited by the family of former Australian Prime Minister Bob Hawke to Sydney where he eventually relocated. Seven years later he moved again, this time to New York City, where he currently teaches Qigong and lives with his wife Dongmei.